All About

CARS

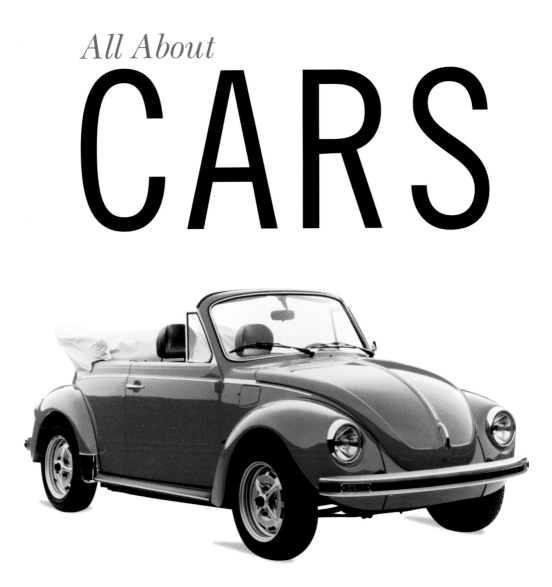

Peter Harrison
CONSULTANT *Peter Cahill*

southwater

This edition is published by Southwater

Southwater is an imprint of Anness Publishing Ltd
Hermes House, 88–89 Blackfriars Road, London SE1 8HA
tel. 020 7401 2077; fax 020 7633 9499
www.southwaterbooks.com; info@anness.com

© Anness Publishing Ltd 2001, 2003

This edition distributed in the UK by The Manning Partnership Ltd,
6 The Old Dairy, Melcombe Road, Bath BA2 3LR;
tel. 01225 478 444; fax 01225 478 440; sales@manning-partnership.co.uk

This edition distributed in the USA and Canada by National Book Network,
4501 Forbes Boulevard, Suite 200, Lanham, MD 20706;
tel. 301 459 3366; fax 301 429 5746; www.nbnbooks.com

This edition distributed in Australia by Pan Macmillan Australia,
Level 18, St Martins Tower, 31 Market St, Sydney, NSW 2000;
tel. 1300 135 113; fax 1300 135 103; customer.service@macmillan.com.au

This edition distributed in New Zealand by The Five Mile Press (NZ) Ltd,
PO Box 33–1071 Takapuna, Unit 11/101–111 Diana Drive, Glenfield, Auckland 10;
tel. (09) 444 4144; fax (09) 444 4518; fivemilenz@xtra.co.nz

Publisher: Joanna Lorenz
Managing Editor, Children's Books: Gilly Cameron Cooper
Assistant Editor: Jenni Rainford
Designer: Sarah Melrose
Copy Editor: Mike Stocks
Photographer: John Freeman
Stylist: Melanie Williams
Picture Researcher: Gwen Campbell
Illustrator: Guy Smith
Editorial Reader: Diane Ashmore
Production Controller: Claire Rae

Previously published as *Investigations Cars*

10 9 8 7 6 5 4 3 2 1

The publishers would like to thank the following
children for modelling in this book:
Katie Appleby, Joseph Brightman, Shaun Liam Cook,
Thomas James, Gabrielle Locke, Emma Molley,
Jamie Pyle, Jasmine Sharland, and Amber-Hollie Wood.

PICTURE CREDITS

CONTENTS

THE JOURNEY BEGINS

CARS MAKE people mobile in a way that would have been impossible only a century ago. Then, a journey by road of just 30 miles could have taken an entire day. Today, we can travel this distance in half an hour. The ability to go where you want, when you want, quickly, makes traveling much easier. Millions of people all over the world use cars to travel to work or to go shopping, to go on vacation and to visit friends and relatives. Horse-drawn carriages and carts, and walking, were the main forms of transportation for thousands of years before cars. Many roads were in poor condition. Because cars moved under their own power, and encouraged better roads, they allowed people to travel much more.

Hold on tight
Very early cars such as this Velo, made in Germany in 1893 by Karl Benz, had no covering bodywork. When Benz's daughter Clara went driving, she sat high above the road with very little to hang on to if the car hit a bump in the road.

By the numbers
The tachometer (rev. counter), speedometer and clock from a Rolls-Royce Silver Ghost have solid brass fittings and glass covers. They were assembled by hand. The instruments on early cars were often made by skilled craftspeople. The Silver Ghost was made continuously from 1906 until 1925.

Bold as brass
A gleaming brass horn and lamp are proud examples of the detailed work that went into making the first cars. Early cars were made with materials that would be far too expensive for most people today. Seats were upholstered with thickly padded leather, because the cars had poor suspension. This prevented the drivers and passengers from being jolted up and down too much.

Old bruiser

This Bentley was built before 1931, when the company was taken over by Rolls-Royce. Bentley built powerful and sturdy sports cars, some weighing up to 775 lbs. They won many motor races in the 1920s and 1930s, such as the Le Mans 24-hour race in France. Big cars such as these were built on heavy metal chassis (frames). They had wood-framed bodies covered in metal and cloth, huge headlights and large, wire-spoked wheels.

Egg on wheels

In the 1950s and 1960s, car makers began to make very small cars, such as this German BMW Isetta. Around 160,000 Isettas were produced between 1955 and 1962. Manufacturers developed small cars because they were cheaper to buy and to run, and used less parking space. The Isetta, like so many of the microcars, was powered by a small motorcycle engine.

Cool cruisin'

Cadillac was an American company known for its stylish designs. This Cadillac from the 1950s, with its large tail fins and shiny chrome, is a typical example. Many cars from the 1950s and 1960s, including this one, are known as classic cars. People like to collect them and restore them to their original condition.

Redhead

The Italian car maker Ferrari has a reputation for making very fast, very expensive cars. This 1985 Testarossa has a top speed of 175 mph. Very few people can afford to own such a car. Even if they have the money, it takes great driving skill to get the best out of one.

Going nowhere?

The success of the car has its downside. Millions of people driving cars causes problems such as traffic jams and air pollution. Also, the building of new roads can ruin the countryside. These issues are being debated all over the world.

THE EARLIEST CARS

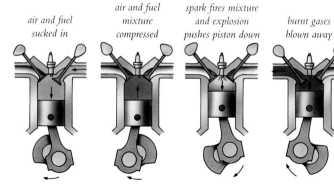

air and fuel sucked in   *air and fuel mixture compressed*   *spark fires mixture and explosion pushes piston down*   *burnt gases blown away*

AMONG THE most important builders of early cars and car engines were the Germans Nikolaus Otto, Karl Benz and Gottlieb Daimler. In the late 1800s, they built the first internal combustion engines and found ways to link the engines to wheels. Car engines are called internal (inside) combustion (burning) engines because they burn a mixture of fuel and air inside a small chamber. People had long been trying to find ways to make engines for road transportation. In 1770, the Frenchman Nicholas-Joseph Cugnot made a steam engine that drove a three-wheeled cart. It was too heavy to use, however, and only two were built. The achievement of Benz, Otto and Daimler was to make a small engine that could generate enough power for road vehicles. In Great Britain, the earliest cars are known as veteran (built before 1905) and Edwardian (built between 1905 and 1919). They were not as reliable as modern vehicles, but sometimes more finely built.

Suck, squeeze, bang, blow
A car's piston (like an unturned metal cup) moves in a rhythm of four steps called the Otto cycle, after Nikolaus Otto. First, it moves down to suck in fuel mixed with air. Then it pushes up and compresses (squeezes) the mixture. The spark plug ignites the fuel. The bang of the explosion pushes the piston down again. When the piston moves up again, it blows out the burnt gases.

Trim trike
The 3-wheeled Benz Motorwagen was first made in 1886. It was steered by a small hand lever on top of a tall steering column. Karl Benz began his career building carriages. He used this training when he built his first car in 1885. By 1888 Benz was employing 50 people to build his Motorwagens.

Follow the leader
Soon after the first cars were being driven on the roads, accidents started to happen. Until 1904, there was a law in Great Britain requiring a person carrying a red flag to walk in front of the car. This forced the car driver to go slowly. The flag was to warn people that a car was coming.

Remember this

Important military gentlemen pose for photos with their cars. They are not in the driving seats, however. They had chauffeurs to drive the cars for them. Car owners in the early 1900s liked to show their cars off. They often posed for photographs to keep for souvenirs.

Look out!

The car horns that early drivers sounded to warn pedestrians were very different than those in modern cars. When the driver squeezed the rubber bulb, air traveled through the tube and made a noise when it came out of the end.

Snow disaster

Early cars were hard to control at times because their braking and steering systems were not very effective. When bad weather such as snow made the ground slippery, the car could easily run off the road. Even in modern cars with efficient brakes and steering, snow-covered roads are still dangerous.

All wrapped up

Drivers at the turn of the century wore thick goggles to protect their eyes, because their cars had no protective bodywork. The roads were not smooth and stones and dust were thrown up by the wheels. Cold winds felt even colder in a moving, open car, so thick caps and heavy driving clothes were worn to keep warm.

Nose to tail horses

This photograph from the late 1800s shows why the British talk about nose-to-tail traffic jams. Before cars were invented, most transportation was by horse-drawn carriage. City streets in those days could become just as jammed with vehicles as they do today.

WHEELS IN MOTION

BEFORE A CAR MOVES, the engine must change the up-and-down movement of the pistons into the round-and-round movement of a shaft (rod) that turns the wheels. With the engine running, the driver presses down the clutch and selects first gear in the gearbox. The engine turns a shaft called a crankshaft. The power from the turning crankshaft is then transmitted through the gearbox to the wheels on the road. The combined movement makes the wheels on the road turn forwards. The wheels turn backwards when the driver pushes the gear stick into reverse gear.

This project shows you how to make a simple machine that creates a similar motion, where one kind of movement that goes round and round can be turned into another kind of movement that goes up and down.

Wind up
The earliest motor cars did not have a starter motor. The driver had to put a starting handle into the front of the car. This connected to the engine's crankshaft to turn it. Turning the handle was hard work and could break the driver's arm if not done correctly. Button-operated starters began to be fitted in 1912.

CHANGING MOTION

You will need: *shoebox, thin metal rod about ¹/8-in. diameter, pliers, jelly jar lid, tape, scissors, 1 thick plastic straw, pencil, piece of stiff paper, at least 4 color felt-tipped pens, 1 thin plastic straw*

1 Place the shoebox narrow-side-down on a flat surface. With one hand push the metal rod through the center, making sure your other hand will not get jabbed by the rod.

2 Bend the rod at right angles where it comes out of the box. Attach the jelly jar lid to it with adhesive tape. Push the lid until it rests against the side of the box.

3 Carefully use the pliers to bend the piece of rod sticking out of the other side of the box. This will make a handle for the piston that will be able to turn easily.

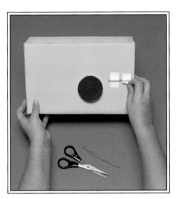

4 Cut a piece of thick plastic straw about 2 in. long and tape it to the side of the box close to the jelly jar lid. Make sure that it just sticks up beyond the edge of the box.

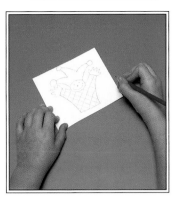

5 Draw a design in pencil on a piece of stiff paper. Copy the jester shown in this project or draw a simple clown. Choose something that looks good when it moves.

6 Using the felt-tipped pens, color the design until it looks the way you want it to. The more colorful the figure is, the nicer it will look on the top of the piston.

7 Carefully cut the finished drawing out of the paper. Make sure you have a clean-edged design. Try not to smudge the felt-tipped color with your fingers.

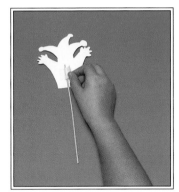

8 Use the tape to attach the thin plastic straw to the bottom of the drawing. About 3/4 in. of straw should be attached.

10 Place the box on end so the jester is at the top. Turn the handle on the left-hand side. As you turn, the jelly jar lid revolves and pushes the jester up and down, like a piston.

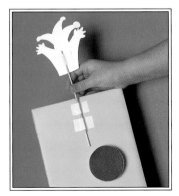

9 Slide the straw attached to the drawing into the straw taped to the back of the box. It will come out of the other end. Push down so that the straw touches the edge of the jelly jar lid.

MASS PRODUCTION

ONCE WAYS had been found to power a small, wheeled road vehicle, more and more people wanted to own a car. Having one made getting around so much easier. However, early cars were built by hand, piece by piece, which took time. In 1903, the inventor Henry Ford produced the Model A Ford, the first car designed to be built in large numbers. It gave him the idea to mass-produce all the separate parts of a car in the same place, then have his workers assemble many cars at the same time. This became known as the production-line method. By 1924, 10 million Ford cars had been built and sold. Today, almost all cars are built on production lines. Robots (automated machines) do much of the work. Some cars are still built by hand, but they can only be built very slowly. For example, the British sports-car maker Morgan made 11 cars a week in 1999. In comparison, the Ford Motor Company built about 138,000 cars a week in the same year.

Tin Lizzie
The Model T Ford was the world's first mass-produced (assembled on a production line) car. Millions were made and sold all over the world. Nowadays people collect examples of these cars, maintaining, restoring and repairing them, often to a gleaming state. It is unlikely that they would have been so well cared for by their original owners.

Herbert's big idea
The Austin Seven was one of the most popular cars ever. This version is a sporting two seater. Between 1922 and 1938 there were many versions, including racing cars and even vans. The Austin Motor Company was founded by Herbert Austin in 1903. The company allowed other car makers to build the Austin Seven in France, Japan, America and Germany.

Beetling about
In 1937, the German government founded a car company to build cheap cars. The car, designed by Dr Ferdinand Porsche, was called the Volkswagen, meaning "people's car", but it gained the nickname of the "Beetle" because of its unusual shape. Some people painted their Beetles for fun. By the 1960s, the car was popular worldwide. By 2000, over 21 million Volkswagens had been sold.

Next one, please

Modern cars are made with the help of machines in factories. Each machine does a different job. Some weld metal parts together, others attach fittings and secure fastenings, others spray paint. The car's metal body parts come together on a moving track that runs past each machine. Making cars like this means they can be put together quickly and in vast numbers.

Big yellow taxi

For people without a car, such as tourists, taxis are a convenient way of getting around in towns and cities. Taxi drivers try to find the best short cuts for an easy journey. Hiring a taxicab also means that people don't have to find a place to park. The bright yellow-colored "checker cabs" in New York became a symbol for the city all over the world, because everyone recognized them.

FACT BOX

• Speedometers (dials showing a car's speed) were first used in cars in 1901.

• The American car maker Buick started life as a bathtub manufacturer.

• By 1936, more than 50 percent of all American families owned a car.

The people's servant

The Trabant was from East Germany. Many millions were built for ordinary people. Its name comes from a Hungarian word meaning "servant", and the Trabant served as a cheap, reliable car across Eastern Europe. This 601 model was first made in 1964.

Alec's big idea

Launched in 1959, the Morris Mini Minor was one of the most revolutionary cars of the last 50 years. It was cheap to buy and cheap to run, easy to drive and easy to park. Despite its small size, it could carry four people comfortably. The car's designer, Alec Issigonis, a British citizen of Greek parentage, also designed the Morris Minor, a budget car launched in 1948.

THE ENGINE

A CAR'S ENGINE is made up of metal parts. They are designed to work together smoothly and efficiently. In older cars, a valve called a carburetor feeds a mixture of air and fuel into the cylinder, where the mixture is burnt to produce power. Newer cars often use an injection system, which measures and controls the amount of fuel into the engine more accurately. To keep the engine cool, water is pumped from the radiator and circulated around chambers in the cylinder block. The waste gases created by the burned fuel are carried away by the exhaust system. The engine sucks in the air and petrol mixture and allows it to burn. To help the moving parts move against each other smoothly, they are lubricated with oil from the engine oil sump. A pump squirts the oil on to the parts.

A car's electrical power is driven by an alternator. The electrical current is stored in the battery. This provides the electricity for the spark that ignites the fuel mixture, for the car's electrical system, and for its heater, lights, radio, windshield wipers and instruments.

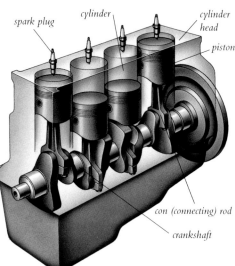

spark plug · cylinder · cylinder head · piston · con (connecting) rod · crankshaft

Working together

Most car engines have four cylinders. In each cylinder a piston moves up and down. Four rods, one from each piston, turn metal joints attached to the crankshaft. As the rods turn the joints, the crankshaft moves round and round. The movement is transmitted to the wheels, using the gearbox to control how fast the wheels turn relative to the engine.

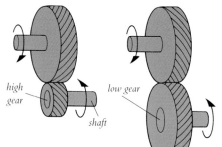

high gear · low gear · shaft

Wheels within wheels

The car's engine turns a shaft (rod) with different sized gears (toothed wheels) on it. High gears are used for more speed because when a big wheel turns a small one, it turns faster. The gear system is called the transmission, because it transmits (moves) the engine's power to the car's wheels. Many cars have five forward gears. The biggest is needed for slow speeds, and the smallest for high speeds. When the car goes round corners, its wheels move at different speeds. A set of gears called the differential allows the wheels to do this.

Turbo tornado

This 1997 Dodge engine can make a car go especially fast because it has a turbocharger that forces the fuel and air mixture faster and more efficiently into the engine cylinder head. Turbochargers are driven by waste exhaust gases drawn away from the exhaust system, which is a way of turning the waste gases to good use. Turbochargers are very effective at boosting engine power.

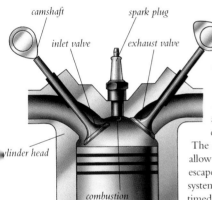

Power control
The distributor has two jobs. It connects and disconnects low-value electric power to the coil. It also supplies high-value electric power from the coil to each spark plug. This makes a spark big enough to ignite the air and fuel mixture at exactly the right time.

lead to spark plug

lead from coil

spark plug contact

rotor arm

contact breaker

What you see is what you get
This vintage racing Bentley displays its twin carburetors mounted on a supercharger (a mechanically driven device similar to a turbocharger) in front of the engine. The water pipes from the radiator to the engine, electric leads, plug leads and large open exhaust pipes can all be seen.

camshaft

spark plug

inlet valve

exhaust valve

cylinder head

combustion chamber

Double movement
The camshaft opens and closes the inlet and exhaust valves. The valves are fitted into the cylinder head, and open and close holes in the combustion chamber. The exhaust valve opens to allow burned waste gases to escape into the car's exhaust system. The spark plug is timed to spark when both valves have closed both holes.

See and be seen
The lights used on early cars usually burned either oil or gas. Oil was carried in a small container in the bottom of the lamp. Gas was created by dissolving in water tablets of carbide (carbon mixed with metal) carried in a canister.

Blow them away
Mercedes-Benz fitted a supercharger to this 1936 540K to add power to the engine. The German company first used superchargers on their racing cars in 1927. This method of adding power had first been used on airplane engines in 1915.

IN THE RIGHT GEAR

GEARS ARE toothed wheels that interlock with each other to transmit circular motion. They have been used in machines of many kinds for over 2,000 years. In a car gearbox, the gears are arranged on shafts so that they mesh with one another when they are selected. Cars have four, five or six forward gears according to the design, use and cost of the car. Several gears are needed because driving requires different combinations of speed and force at different times.

The largest gear wheel is first gear and turns slower than the higher gears. It provides more force and less speed for when the car is moving from stop, or going uphill. In fifth gear, less force and more speed is provided. This gear wheel is the smallest and rotates the fastest. The project connects two gears to show the beautiful patterns that gears can make. Then you can make your own three-gear machine.

Uphill struggle
Pushing a car up a steep hill in a 1920s car rally put a lot of strain on the low gears in a car. On steep slopes, first and second gears are often the only ones that a driver can use. Fourth gear is used for flat roads and fifth gear for cruising at high speeds.

DRAWING WITH GEARS

You will need: compass, 8½ x 11-in. sheet of white paper, black pen, scissors, 8½ x 11-in. sheet of thin cardboard, two strips of corrugated cardboard, tape, 3 colored felt-tipped pens.

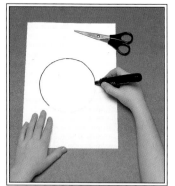

1 Using the compass, trace a 5½-in. diameter circle on the paper. Draw over it with the pen and cut it out. On the cardboard, trace, draw and cut out another circle with a diameter of 4½ in.

2 Tape corrugated cardboard around the circles, as shown. Make a hole in the small circle wide enough for the tip of a felt-tipped pen. Turn the small wheel inside the larger. Trace the path in felt-tipped pen.

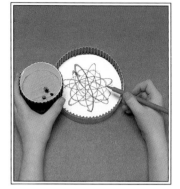

3 Make a second hole in the small wheel. Turn the small gear inside the larger using another felt-tipped pen. Make a third hole in the small wheel and use a third color pen to create an exciting geometric design.

THREE-GEAR MACHINE

You will need: compass, 8¹/2 x 11-in. sheet of cardboard, pen, scissors, 3 strips of corrugated card, tape, 8¹/2 x 11-in. piece of fiberboard, glue, 2¹/2-in. piece of ¹/2-in. diameter wood dowel, three push pins.

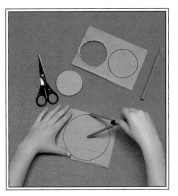

1 Use the compass to trace one 5¹/2-in. diameter and two 4¹/2-in. diameter circles in the cardboard. Draw around the circle edges with the pen and cut the circles out.

2 Carefully wrap the strips of corrugated cardboard around the circles, using one strip per circle, corrugated side out. Tape each strip to the bottom of the circles.

3 Place the largest gear wheel on the piece of fiberboard. Hold the gear down and glue the dowel onto the side of the gear base at the edge of the wheel. Set aside until it is dry.

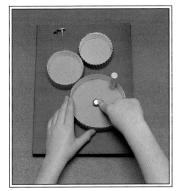

4 Position all three gears on the fiberboard, edges just touching each other. Pin each of them firmly to the fiberboard with a push pin but allow them to turn.

6 Now you have a three-gear machine where the energy from each gear is being transferred to the other, just like the gears in a car.

5 Gently turn the dowel on the largest gear. As that gear turns, the two others that are linked together by the corrugated cardboard will turn against it. See how they move in opposite directions to each other.

SAFE RIDE AND HANDLING

MOST MODERN cars have four wheels. The wheels tend to be placed one at each corner, which helps to distribute the car's weight evenly on the road. An evenly balanced car rides and handles well and has good road grip and braking. Engine power usually drives either the front or rear wheels. However, with the growth in off-road driving in farming and for pleasure, all-wheel drive has become increasingly popular. Driving safely at high speed in a straight line or round corners is a test of how well a car has been designed. Many cars now have power-assisted steering to make steering easier. Tires are an important part of good road handling. The tread pattern and grooves are designed to make the tire grip the road efficiently, especially in wet, slippery conditions.

Big bopper
The French tire manufacturer Michelin has been making tires since 1888. The Michelin brand has been known for many years by the symbol of a human figure that looks as though it is made out of tires.

Gripping stuff
Tire tread patters have raised pads, small grooves and water-draining channels to grip the road surface. There are different kinds of tires for cars, buses, trucks and tractors. Tire makers also make tires for different road conditions. Examples include winter tires and special self-sealing tires that stay hard even when they are damaged.

Dig deep
Tractor tires are very deeply grooved. This allows them to grip well in slippery mud. The width of the tires spreads the weight of the heavy vehicle over soft ground. The tires are high so that the tractor can ride easily over obstacles such as big rocks on the ground.

Burn the rubber

Race car tires are wide so that the car can go as fast as possible while maintaining grip and stability on the road. They are made in various very hard mixtures of rubber to cope with different amounts of heat generated by racing in different conditions. Ordinary tires would melt.

Out for a spin

Until very light alloy wheels became available in the last 20 years, sports cars often had wire-spoke wheels. These combined strength with lightness, which are both important features in a sports car. When a sports car brakes or turns sharply, modern wire-spoke wheels are strong enough to take the strain.

pinion *shaft from steering wheel* *rack*

Keeping control

A driver turns the car's front wheels left or right by turning the steering wheel. The pinion mechanism at the bottom of the steering shaft engages with a toothed rack. This is connected to the wheels by means of a system of joints and wheels. As the steering wheel turns, the movement of the pinion along the rack turns the road wheels.

Monster trucks

Very large trucks that carry heavy loads use enormous tires to spread the weight. This flatbed truck has been equipped with earth-mover tires for fun. Look how much bigger they are than the car the truck's rolling over.

Strong grip

Traveling at high speed on a wet road can be dangerous. Water can form a film that is able to lift a tire clear of the road surface for several seconds. To prevent this, tire makers mold drain channels into the tire's tread to push the water away from under the tire as it rotates.

SPEED CONTESTS

R ACE CARS against one another to test their speed and endurance has gone on for over 100 years. The American car maker Henry Ford, for example, designed and built race cars before he set up the Ford car factory in 1903. Many kinds of car races now take place, including stock-car, rally, speedway and drag racing. The FIA (*Fédération Internationale de l'Automobile*) makes rules about issues such as the tracks, the design and power of the cars, and the safety of drivers and spectators.

The fastest and most powerful kind of track racing is Formula One, also known as Grand Prix racing. The cars can travel up to 200 mph on straight sections of track. Because the races are so exciting, the best drivers are paid in the millions. Formula One winners, such as David Coulthard and Michael Schumacher, are international celebrities. Technological advances in production-line cars have often been developed and tested in Grand Prix cars.

GRAND-PRIX Dieppe
de l'A·C·F· 1907
NAZZARO au F·I·A·T·

Your move
When racing drivers complete a race and cross the finishing line, a race official waves a black and white flag known as the checkered flag. The black-and-white pattern of squares on the finishing flag looks like the pattern on a chessboard. It is known all over the world as the sign of motor racing.

Monster motors
Early Grand Prix cars, such as this 10.2 liter Fiat, had enormous engines. Grand Prix racing began in France in 1904 and slowly spread to other countries. The *Association Internationale des Automobiles Clubs Reconnus* (AIACR) set the rules for races until it was reformed as the FIA in 1946.

Furious Ferrari
The Italian car maker Ferrari has been making race cars since 1940. Here the German Michael Schumacher, driving the Ferrari F399, rounds a curve on the 7¹/₂-mi.-Catalunya circuit at the 1999 Barcelona Grand Prix.

FACT BOX

• Between 1980 and 1982, the French driver Alain Prost won 51 Formula One races, the highest number so far achieved by any Grand Prix driver.

• Ayrton Senna won the Monaco Grand Prix a record six times between 1987 and 1993.

• The racetrack at Indianapolis, Indiana, was known as "the brickyard" because it was paved with bricks until 1961.

Take-off

The speeds at which rally cars travel means they often fly over the tops of the hills on the course. The driver and navigator of this car in the 1999 Portuguese Rally are strapped into their seats to protect them from the tremendous thump that will come when the car's four wheels touch the ground in a second or two.

Take it to the limit

The heat generated by a Top Fuel drag racer's engine at the 1996 NHRA (*National Hot Rod Association*) Winternational makes the air vibrate around it. Drag races are short, like sprint races for athletes. The races take place over a straight course only 400 yds long, and the cars can reach speeds of 250 mph. The flat spoilers on the front and rear of the cars are pushed down by the air rushing past, helping to keep the car on the road.

The chase

Tight bends are a test of driving skills for Formula One drivers. The cars brake hard from very high speeds as they approach the bend. Drivers try not to leave any gap that following cars could use for overtaking. As the drivers come out of the bend they accelerate as hard as is possible without skidding and going into a spin.

Making a splash

Rally car driving is extremely tough on the cars and on the drivers. Cars drive over deserts, mud-filled roads, rivers, snow and many other obstacles. The cars follow the same route, but start at different times. The course is divided into separate sections known as Special Stages. There is a time limit for each stage. The winner of the rally is the car which has the fastest overall time.

Thrill becomes spill

The Brazilian Mauricio Gugelmin's car soars into the air at the 1985 French Grand Prix, crashing to the ground upside down. The driver survived and has since taken part in 74 Grand Prix races. Safety regulations have improved in recent years.

RACE TRACKS

PEOPLE HAVE been racing cars on specially designed public circuits (tracks) almost since cars were invented. The first race on a special circuit took place in 1894 in France. The Italian track at Monza is one of the oldest racing circuits. It was built for the 1922 Italian Grand Prix. Among the most well-known tracks are Silverstone and Brands Hatch in Great Britain, Indianapolis in the United States, the Nürburgring in Germany, and Monaco. Millions of people all over the world watch the races at these tracks and on television. The teams and the drivers compete furiously with one another to prove whose car is the fastest or can keep driving the longest. Sometimes the competition can be so fierce it is deadly. Ayrton Senna, a top Brazilian racing driver, died in a fatal crash at Imola in Italy in 1994. In this project, you can build your own race track, specially designed to let your cars build up speed on a steep slope, and race against a partner to see whose car is the fastest.

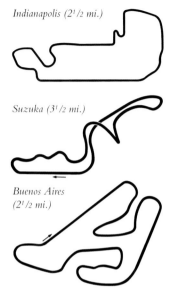

Indianapolis (2¹/2 mi.)

Suzuka (3¹/2 mi.)

Buenos Aires (2¹/2 mi.)

TESTING GROUND

You will need: *10 in. of 3-in.-diameter cardboard tube, scissors, small paintbrush, blue paint, 10 strips of colored paper 2¹/2 x ³/4 in., tape, 2 strips of white paper ¹/2 x 3 in., pencil, red and black felt-tipped pen, pieces of colored and white paper, toothpicks, 8¹/2 x 11-in. sheet of stiff red card stock, ruler, 2 small model cars.*

Twist and turn
All racetracks, such as those shown above, test the skill of the drivers and the speed and handling of the racing cars. They combine curves with straight stretches. Sharp curves are known as hairpin curves. Most tracks are between 2¹/2 and 3¹/2 mi. in length.

1 Use the scissors to carefully cut the cardboard tube in half along its length. Hold the tube in one hand but make sure you keep the scissor blades away from your hands.

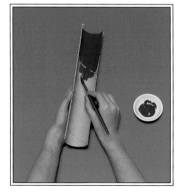

2 Use the paintbrush to apply a thick coat of blue paint to the insides of both halves of the tube. For a more intense color, paint a second coat after the first has dried.

3 Use tape to stick the ten narrow strips of colored paper together. Tape them along their widths to make a flexible seam. This joins the racetrack together.

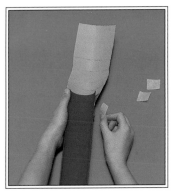

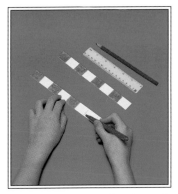

4 Now take the flexible curve you have made from strips of paper. Tape it to one end of one of the painted halves of the tube. Use small pieces of tape.

5 Use a pencil to mark eight equal 1/2-in. strips on both of the strips of white paper. Color in alternate red blocks with a felt-tipped pen to make striped crash barriers.

6 Color in a 1 1/2 x 3-in. piece of paper with 1/2-in. black and white squares. Cut the other paper pieces into pennants (forked flags). Tape the flags to toothpicks.

9 Tape the second half of the tube to the end of the flexible curve. Put in the crash barriers. Now you are ready to roll your toy car down the death–defying slope of your racetrack. Make another racetrack with a friend and you can race each other's cars.

7 Cut three 3-in.-wide strips from the sheet of stiff card stock. Use scissors to cut a semicircle out of the top of each of the strips.

8 Measure with a ruler and cut the three strips to varying heights of 8 in., 5 1/2 in. and 2 3/4 in. Tape them to the bottom of half of the tube, fitting them on at the semicircle shapes to support the half tube in a gradual slope.

Popping the cork
Race winners Canadian Jacques Villeneuve and Frenchman Jean Alesi celebrate by showering each other with champagne at the Luxembourg Grand Prix in 1997.

COLLECTING

The cars that were made many years ago have not been forgotten. In Great Britain, they are known as veteran (made before 1905), Edwardian (1905–1919), vintage (1919–1930) and classic (1930 onward). Enthusiasts (people with a special interest) all over the world collect and maintain old cars. They value them for many reasons, such as the great care that went into making them, their design, their engine power and their rarity. Clubs such as the AACA (Antique Automobile Club of America) and FIVA (*Fédération Internationale Véhicules Anciens*) exist for the collectors of old American and European cars. There are also specific clubs for owners of particular models of car. Owners like to meet up and compare notes on maintaining their vehicles. Their clubs organize tours and rallies in which owners can drive their cars in working order.

Annual get-together
English veteran cars (built before 1905) parade along the sea front in Brighton, England. The London-to-Brighton veteran car run has been held every year (apart from during the wars) since 1904. It celebrates cars being driven without someone with a red flag walking in front to warn of their approach.

Who stole the roof?
Early vehicles were built on the frames of horse-drawn wagons, so they had little protective bodywork. Drivers and their passengers had to wrap up well when driving.

Room for two?
Frenchman Louis Delage built cars of great engineering skill. The engine of this 1911 racing model was so big that there was little room for the driver. The huge tube under the hood carried exhaust gases to the back of the car.

High roller

The Rolls-Royce Silver Ghost is one of the great early vintage cars. It was first built in 1906. Almost 8,000 were made before production finally stopped in 1925. By that time, fewer people were able to afford such large, expensive cars. Individual buyers could have the car's specification and equipment altered according to their own needs. Several Silver Ghosts were produced as armored cars to protect top British Army generals during World War I.

Mighty midget

The 1930 MG Midget was a powerful small car and clearly deserved its name. The Midget was the first car that the MG company sold in large numbers. Its success allowed the firm to expand and become more widely known.

Mint condition

The owners of old cars have to give a great deal of loving care to the car engines. Keeping an original MG Midget engine running demands patience in finding spare parts, maintaining old metal and making regular tests.

Star car

Only 36 Duesenberg cars were built, so whoever owns one now is very lucky. This machine is immediately recognizable as a 1933 Model SJ Speedster because of the engine exhaust tubes coming out from under the hood.

In demand

A 1930s race car combines style and power, qualities that still give Alfa Romeo its strong reputation. Collectors today value race cars of the past just as much as old passenger cars. The Italian car maker Alfa Romeo has been building fast cars since 1915.

Starry Ferrari

The Italian company Ferrari is one of the world's greatest car makers. Owning a Ferrari has always been seen as a symbol of wealth and success, so the cars are favorites with film stars and sports stars. This 166 Ferrari is from the late 1940s.

OFF-ROAD VEHICLES

M OST CARS are designed for driving on smooth roads. There are specialized vehicles, however, that can drive across rough conditions such as mud, desert and rocky terrain. Usually called off-road vehicles (ORVs) or All-Terrain Vehicles (ATVs), cars of this kind often have four-wheel drive, large tires and tough suspensions. They stand high off the ground and have strong bodywork. The earliest ORVs were the American Jeep and the British Land Rover. The Jeep, made by Ford and Willys, started life in World War II. It was designed to travel across roads damaged by warfare. The Land Rover, built by the Rover company in the late 1940s, was based on the idea of the Jeep. It was intended for farmers, who have to drive across difficult terrain. The Land Rover proved useful in all parts of the world where roads were poor or non-existent. Traveling off-road is still a necessity in many places. But in recent times, it has become a popular leisure activity for some drivers, who like to test their driving skills in difficult terrain.

Seaside fun
Driving on beaches is difficult because wheels can sink into the wet sand. Vehicles for driving on beaches are built to be very light, with balloon tires to spread the vehicle's weight over a wide area.

Tough cookie
At the start of World War II the United States Army developed a vehicle with a sturdy engine, body and chassis. The wheels were at the corners for stability over rough ground. The GP (General Purpose) vehicle became known as the Jeep.

No traffic jams
The Lunar Rover, carried to the Moon by *Apollo 17* in 1971, was powered by electricity. The low gravity of the moon meant that it would not sink into soft ground. A wide track and long wheelbase stopped it from turning over if it hit a rock.

Angel of mercy
Vehicles such as Jeeps help doctors to take medical aid to people living in remote areas where there are few roads. A four-wheel drive vehicle, it can cross shallow rivers and rough terrain. A specially strong underbody protects against damage from water.

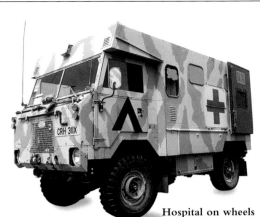

Hospital on wheels
Aid agencies such as UNICEF and *Mèdecins Sans Frontières* use specially adapted trucks equipped as mobile hospitals. They help to save lives in times of war and natural disaster. Heavily reinforced bodywork protects patients and fragile medical supplies.

Electric caddies
A typical game of golf involves traveling 3 mi. or more. Golfers need an easy way to carry heavy golf clubs around the course. Golf carts (also called golf buggies) are simple, light vehicles powered by electricity. They have enough battery life to carry golfers and their clubs from the first to the last hole on the course.

Get tracking
Half-tracks played an important part in World War II, and still do in modern warfare. They have tank tracks in the rear to allow them to travel over very broken surfaces such as roads filled with shell holes and debris. The wheels at the front give half-tracks added mobility that tanks do not have.

Big boss
Large, high, sports-utility cars such as the Mitsubishi Shogun and commercial SUVs grew increasingly popular from the 1980s. They had four-wheel drive, which made driving on rough ground much easier.

CUSTOM-BUILT

Sometimes serious car enthusiasts decide to adapt a standard model. They might alter the engine to make it run faster, or change the body to make it look different. Specially adapted cars like this are known as custom cars. Custom cars have become very popular since the 1950s, particularly in the United States. The wheels may be taken from one kind of car, the body from a second, the mudguards and engine from others, and the different parts are combined to make a completely original car. The end result can be dramatic. These unusual cars have many different names, such as mean machines, street machines, muscle machines and hot rods. Racing custom cars is a popular activity. Stock cars are production-line cars modified slightly for races. Drag racers are incredibly fast and powerful cars built for high speed races over short distances.

Water baby
Surf's up and the muscle machine is on the beach. This cool dude has fitted big, wide tires on a sports car body to spread the car's weight on soft sand. He has been busy with a paintbrush, too, adding flames to his body paint.

Made to order
This car is a mixture of styles. The driver's cab and steering wheel have been made to look like those in a veteran car. The modern engine is chrome-plated, with all the parts visible. The exhaust-outlet tubes resemble those from a 1930s race car. The front wheels are bigger than the rear ones.

Soft furnishings
Some people change the insides of their cars to create a truly luxurious look. They replace the standard features, for example, with soft leather seats, padded dashboards and chrome-covered gear shifts.

Really smokin'
The grille on the hood of a customized hot rod is the turbocharger. It can boost the engine to speeds of 250 mph. When the car brakes at high speed, its tires make lots of smoke because they are burning from friction with the road.

FLUFFY DICE

You will need: square box at least 4¹/₂ in. square, 2 8¹/₂ x 11-in. sheets of white paper, tape, scissors, 7³/₄-in. length of string, 31-in. square of furry fabric, pencil, awl, glue, circle stencil.

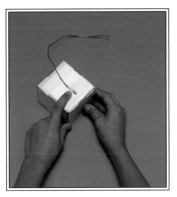

1 Stick white paper around all six surfaces of the box with tape. Use a small piece of tape to stick 1¹/₄ in. of the end of the length of string to one side of the box.

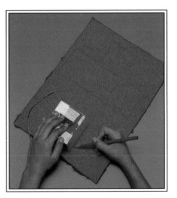

2 Place the fabric furry-side down. Place the box at one edge and draw around it. Then roll the box over and draw around it again. Do six squares like this to form a cross.

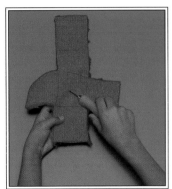

3 Cut out the cross shape. With an awl, carefully make a hole in the fur. Place the box face down on the fur where the string is attached. Pull the string through the hole.

4 Spread glue evenly on the inside of each square of the fabric, one at a time. Press the glued material squares on to the box faces.

5 Choose a medium-sized circle shape from the circle stencil. Using a pencil, draw 21 of the same circles on the piece of white paper.

6 Cut out the circles. Glue them on to the furry side of the fabric. Put six dots on one face, five dots on the next, then four, three, two and finally one dot. You could use a real dice to see the correct arrangement.

7 Make a second dice and hang them in the car for fun. Put them in a place where they will not distract the driver. They should not hang on any of the windows.

UNUSUAL DESIGNS

CARS ARE often adapted (have their design changed) to suit different needs, or just for fun. Three-wheeled cars, a kind of microcar, are cheap to operate and take up less road space than the conventional four-wheeled cars.

Amphibious vehicles that can operate on land and water were built in World War II for fighting. Since then, specialized German, British and Chinese manufacturers have gone on building small numbers of these cars for use in regions with many rivers.

Films studios often create sensational special effects around cars that appear to have special powers. Then there are the real but completely wacky cars, made by people who want to create cars that defy the imagination. These have included cars that split down the middle, cars that are covered in fur, and cars that look like sofas and hot dogs.

Frog face
The microcars produced in in the 1950s and 1960s were for driving in towns. This 1959 Messerschmitt had a tiny engine and was just 9 ft long. Even so, it had a top speed of 65 mph. The top of the car swings over to allow the driver entry. The car was also very cheap to operate. It used only one gallon of gas every 60 mi., almost half the fuel consumption of an average modern car.

Garden car
This car may look like a garden shed, but in order to travel on a public road it needs to conform to all the regulations of the road. It will have passed an annual inspection for safety and road-worthiness. Headlights, turn signals and safety belts are all installed.

Supermarket beep
A giant supermarket cart has been constructed and fitted with a car engine. This vehicle is strictly for fun. Lacking basic safety features such as proper seats, lights and bumpers, it is not allowed to be driven on public roads.

Only in the movies
The 1977 James Bond film, *The Spy Who Loved Me*, featured a car that behaved as though it was also a submarine. It was a British Lotus Elite car body specially altered to create the illusion.

Magic car
Ian Fleming, the creator of James Bond, also wrote a book about a magic car. This became the 1968 film *Chitty Chitty Bang Bang*. The car was an old one that the book's hero, Caractacus Potts, discovered in a junkyard. After restoring it, he discovered it could fly and float.

Kit car
This 3-wheeler Triking, a modern replica (copy) of a 1930s Morgan, is a kit car that has been put together. The owner is supplied with all the different body panels and engine parts, and builds the complete car. Kit cars are cheaper than production-line cars, because the costs of assembly and labor are saved.

FACT BOX

• One of the amphibious vehicles used in World War II was called a "duck" after the initials DUKW given it by the manufacturer, General Motors. It had six wheels and moved through the water powered by a propeller.

• Microcars, such as the BMW Isetta and the Heinkel Trojan, were also known in the 1950s and 1960s as bubble cars because of their round shapes and large window spaces.

• Race tracks such as Le Mans in France, and Monza in Italy, hosted race meetings in the 1950s and 1960s where microcars such as the British Berkeley and the Italian Fiat Bianchina raced against each other.

Web-toed drivers
Cars that can cross water are useful, especially in places where there are rivers but no bridges. Between 1961 and 1968, the German Amphicar company made almost 4,000 amphibious cars. They could reach a speed of 7 mph in the water, pushed along by two small propellers. On land they could reach 70 mph.

COOLING SYSTEM

THE EXPLOSIONS in a car's engine, and the friction caused by its moving parts, create a great deal of heat. If the heat were not kept down, the engine would stop working. The metal parts would expand, seize up and stop. To cool the engine, water from a radiator is pumped through chambers in the cylinder block. The moving water carries heat away from the hottest parts of the engine. The radiator has to be cooled down too. A fan blows air onto it, to cool the water inside. The fan is driven by a belt from the engine crankshaft pulley. This project shows you how to transfer the energy of turning motion from one place to another. It uses a belt to move five reels. In the same way, some of the turning motion of an engine is transferred by a fan belt to the fan.

Rear engine

The air-cooled rear-engined Volkswagen Beetle was designed with an aerodynamic front and no need for a front-mounted radiator. Instead, the engine is cooled by a fan driven by a fan belt, like the one shown here. Engines of this kind are useful in cold climates, where low temperatures can freeze water in radiators.

FAN BELT

You will need: *ruler, 6¹/4-in. square of thin cloth, scissors, 5 spools of thread, 8¹/2 x 11-in. wooden board, glue or glue stick, pencil, 5 flat-headed nails 1¹/2-in. in length, hammer, 3-ft length of 1-in.-wide velvet ribbon, tape, compass, 5 pieces of 6-in.-square colored card stock, 5 wooden skewers.*

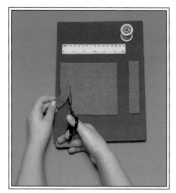

1 Using the ruler, measure five 1-in.-wide strips on the thin cloth. The height of the spools of thread should be more than 1 in. Use the scissors to cut out each strip.

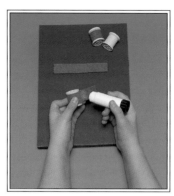

2 Wrap one of the fabric strips around each of the five spools. Glue each strip at the end so that it sits firmly around the spool and does not come loose.

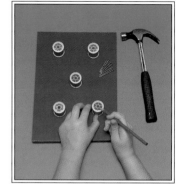

3 Place the spools on the wooden board as shown above. Trace the outlines with a pencil. Put the nails through the center of the spools and carefully hammer them into the board.

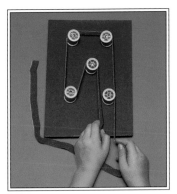

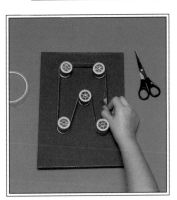

Use the compass to draw circles about 2³/4 in. in diameter on the

4 Wind the ribbon around the spools with the velvet side against four of the spools. Cut the ribbon at the point where you can join both ends round the fifth spool.

5 Tape the two ends of the ribbon together firmly. Make sure that the ribbon wraps firmly around all of the five spools, but not so tightly that it can not move.

6 Use the compass to draw circles about 2³/4 in. in diameter on the pieces of colored card stock. Then draw freehand spiral shapes inside each circle.

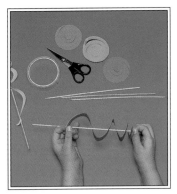

10 Now you are ready to turn the belt. Like a fan belt in a car, it turns the fans around. This is a five-fan machine. You can add more fans if you like.

7 Use the scissors to cut each spiral out of each of the pieces of colored card stock. Start from the outside edge and gradually work your way in along the lines of the spiral.

8 Tape one end of the spiral to the end of a skewer. Wind the other end of the spiral around the skewer a few times. Tape it close to the opposite end of the skewer.

9 Put a small amount of tape on the end of each skewer. Place each skewer into one of the empty holes in the top of each spool of thread.

ENVIRONMENT MATTERS

Cars are convenient, but their effect on the environment causes concern. The manufacture and the driving of cars both use up precious natural resources such as metals and oil. The emissions (waste gases) that gas–powered cars produce pollute the atmosphere. One of them, carbon monoxide, is thought by many scientists to be contributing to problems such as global warming (the warming of the world's climate because of gases trapped in the atmosphere).

Although the environmental problems associated with cars are many, car makers have made many improvements to their models during recent years. Cars are much lighter than they used to be, so smaller amounts of raw materials are needed to make them. Because of their lighter weight, and improvements in their engine efficiency, they can drive many more miles per gallon of fuel than previously. In many countries, the emission of carbon monoxide into the atmosphere is actually lower now than twenty years ago, despite their being many more cars.

Costly accident
The gasoline that cars burn is extracted from oil pumped out of the ground or from under the sea. The oil is transported in enormous ships to refineries where the gasoline is extracted. Occasionally, a tanker sinks or springs a leak. When this happens, oil seeps into the sea and forms a slick on the surface, killing and injuring fish and birds.

FACT BOX

• Ford launched the Ford Ka in 1998, and the Ford Fiesta in 1976. Both are small everyday cars. But the exhaust gases of the 1976 Ford Fiesta contained fifty times more pollutants such as carbon monoxide and nitrogen oxides than the 1998 Ford Ka.

Traffic reports
Traffic police may gradually be replaced by computerized technology called Telematics. In-car navigation systems and traffic messaging (radio messages on traffic conditions) enable drivers to use the best route. This can reduce journey times, and gasoline consumption, by 10 percent.

Going nowhere fast

There are too many cars in the world. Traffic congestion is a common experience for many. Transportation experts are trying to link public transportation with car use to reduce the problem. For example, park-and-ride schemes allow drivers to park near a town, then catch a free bus downtown.

Rubber bounces back

The treads (gripping patterns) on tires wear away until the tire is too smooth to grip the road. Car owners throw away the old tires and buy new ones. Like metal and plastic, rubber does not bio-degrade (decay naturally) easily. Tires can be reused by being shredded and turned into tiny chips of rubber. These can be melted down to make asphalt for covering roads.

Plug-in car

Electric cars create much less pollution than gas-powered cars. They use electricity stored in batteries. The batteries need to be recharged regularly by being plugged into the main electricity supply. In parts of California, drivers can find recharging stations in public places. Seven hours of charging will allow a car to travel a distance of about 100 mi.

In the dump

Most of the materials used in cars can be recycled. Car companies are using more and more recycled materials in their new cars, such as old batteries to make new batteries, and plastic accessories to make new plastic-based parts. But it is still very expensive to recycle the metal, so many old cars end up in the dump.

Lights in the smog

Fumes from cars cause smog over the city of Los Angeles. This is dangerous to people's health. Scientists are constantly researching alternative fuels. CNG (compressed natural gas) cars, which are already on sale, produce 20 percent fewer emissions than gas-powered cars.

BRAKING SYSTEMS

CARS HAVE two types of brakes. Parking brakes lock the rear wheels when the car is standing still. They are controlled by the handbrake lever inside the car. Brakes used when the car is moving are usually made of steel discs attached to each wheel. They are called disc brakes and are controlled by the brake pedal inside the car. The disc brakes attached to the car's road wheels work just like the model disc brake in the project. Putting the brakes on too sharply when a car is moving can cause a skid, when the wheels lock and the tires slide on the road surface.

Antilock braking systems (ABS), now used in many cars, measure the road surface conditions and stop the car from going into a skid. This is done by making the disc brakes turn on and off very quickly, so that the wheels cannot lock.

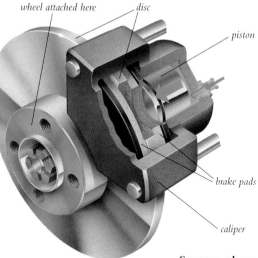

wheel attached here   disc

piston

brake pads

caliper

Squeeze, please

The disc brake unit's disc is attached to a turning hub. This is bolted to the road wheel. When the driver presses the brake pedal, fluid is squeezed down a tube to the piston on the side of the disc brake. The piston presses together two pads, one on either side of the disc, gripping it firmly and stopping it from turning. As the disc slows, so does the car wheel.

Ready, set, go
A stock car (modified production-line car) speeds up from stop very quickly. The driver builds up the power in the engine. When the engine is near full power, the driver quickly releases the brakes. Because the wheels suddenly start spinning incredibly quickly, the tires roar and whine against the hard ground, and burn with the heat of the friction (rubbing) against the road. The burning rubber turns into smoke which billows in dark clouds around the rear wheels.

Water sports
Rally drivers have to deal with extreme conditions such as dirt tracks, mud, snow and water. Powerful brakes help them to keep control of the cars. After going through water, a rally car's brakes would be wet. This makes them less effective because there is less friction. The brake pads slip against the wet disc. The driver has to press the brake pedal with a pumping action to get rid of the water.

DISC BRAKE

You will need: *scissors, 16-in. length of fabric, circular cardboard box with lid, tape, pencil, 8-in. length of ¼-in. diameter wood dowel, glue, 3 x 5-in. piece of medium sandpaper, 2½ x 4-in. wood block, two plastic cups, insulation tape.*

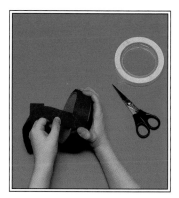

1 Use the scissors to cut a 16-in. long strip from the fabric. You may have to use special fabric cutting scissors if ordinary scissors are not sharp enough.

2 Take the strip of fabric you have cut out and wrap it around the rim of the circular cardboard box. Secure it firmly in place with small pieces of tape.

6 Spin the lid fast on the dowel. As it spins, bring the sandpaper into contact with the edge of the lid and see how it stops the lid turning. Test your brake disc and see how quickly and how gradually you can stop the lid.

3 Make a hole in the center of the box's lid with a pencil. Twist the pencil until it pierces the bottom of the box. Now gently push the wood dowel through both holes.

4 Spread lots of glue onto the sandpaper's smooth side. Wrap the sandpaper carefully over the top of the wood block, pressing to attach it.

5 Stand two plastic cups upside down on a flat surface. Rest either end of the wooden dowel on each cup. Cut two small pieces of insulation tape. Use them to attach each end of the dowel firmly to the cup tops.

SAFETY ISSUES

TRAFFIC ACCIDENTS are a constant danger. As the number of cars on the roads increased in the first half of the 1900s, the number of accidents to pedestrians and drivers increased also. During the last fifty years, ideas were put forward to reduce the scale of the problem. Gradually, most countries have decided that a driver must pass a test in driving skills. Governments have created safety regulations for road builders and car makers to follow. In many places, drivers and passengers are required by law to wear seat belts, and driving while under the influence of alcohol is forbidden in most countries.

New cars often have built-in safety features such as car body parts that resist crushing, and airbags that inflate to lessen the impact of collisions. Emergency road services deal more quickly with injured people. All these advances mean that in many countries there are now fewer road deaths than there were twenty years ago, even though there are more cars.

Safe and sound
If a car traveling at the relatively slow speed of 20 mph stopped suddenly, a child could be thrown forward and injured. To prevent this, a child can be strapped into a specially designed chair or seat that is fixed securely to a car seat. It also stops the child from distracting the driver.

Bags of life
Experts who test cars for safety use crash-test dummies that react just like human bodies. These dummies are being protected by airbags, which were introduced into European production-line cars by Volvo in the 1980s. Airbags act as a kind of life-saving cushion, protecting a person from being thrown into the dashboard or the seat in front. The airbags inflate with gases as soon as sensors detect the first moment of a collision.

Not a care in the world
In the early days of driving, people were much less aware of road safety as there were very few cars. In this 1906 drawing, a rich young man-about-town leans over the back of his car seat. He does not have to worry about where he is going because he has a chauffeur to drive him. Yet even the chauffeur is careless and narrowly avoids hitting a pedestrian in front of the car.

Pain in the neck

When a car stops suddenly, a person's head is jolted forward and then sharply backward. This can cause damage to the neck called whiplash. It often results in serious injury. Car manufacturers have invented seats that slide backward and then tilt. The pictures show (1) the seat in normal position, (2) the seat sliding back, and (3) the seat's backrest tilting over. Combined with the headrest at the top, this seat design helps reduce whiplash.

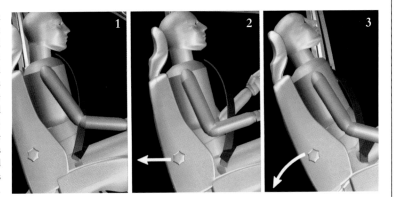

Traffic control

Before traffic control measures were introduced, accidents were common. In 1914, the first electric traffic light was installed in Cleveland, Ohio. Traffic lights control the flow of cars through intersections.

Grand slam

When cars collide with each other at high speed their bodywork (outer metal shell) smashes and twists. Safety engineers test the strength of a car's bodywork by hitting sample cars with powerful robot sleds. Wires attached to the car detect information about safety weak points. This information is used to improve the safety of materials and designs used in cars.

Major obstruction ahead

When a large truck tips over and spills its cargo, it creates all kinds of problems. Fire crews rescue anyone who is trapped in a vehicle, and medical teams treat any injured people. The police and fire crews direct the removal of the spilled cargo. Heavy cranes are needed to shift the truck. Although drivers are diverted to other roads, traffic jams build up that can stretch for long distances.

GOOD DESIGN

CAR MAKERS use large teams of people to create their new cars. Designers, design engineers and production engineers combine with the sales team to develop a car that people will want to buy. But before the new car is announced to the public, models are made. A quarter-sized clay model is tested in a wind tunnel to investigate the car's aerodynamics (how air flows over its shape). Finally, a prototype (early version) of the car is built and tested for road handling, engine quality and comfort.

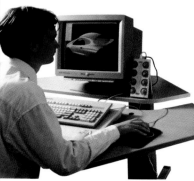

Sleek and shiny
CAD (computer-aided design) software allows car designers to create a 3-dimensional image of a new car design that can be looked at from any angle.

Painting on wheels
An old Mini Minor has been painted in exciting bright designs.

MODEL CAR

***You will need:** 2 8¹/2 x 11-in. sheets of cardboard, scissors, glue, brush, awl, 6-in. square piece of colored card stock, pliers, 4 paper clips, 2 x 4-in. lengths of ¹/2-in. diameter wood dowel, tape.*

Wire basket
Three-dimensional, wire-frame (see-through) computer images allow designers to see how the shapes of the car fit together.

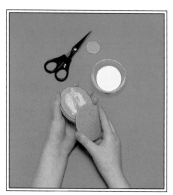

1 Cut out four 1-in. and eight 2¹/2-in. diameter cardboard circles. Glue the 2¹/2-in. circles together to make four wheels. Glue a 1-in. circle to the center of each wheel.

2 Use the awl to make a hole in the center of each wheel. Cut four ¹/8-in. strips of colored card stock. Wrap one around each of the wheel rims. Glue the overlapping ends.

3 Push straightened paper clips into the holes and bend the ends with the pliers. Attach the wheels to the two pieces of dowel by pushing the paper clips into the ends.

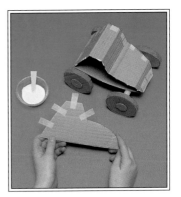

4 Cut a piece of cardboard to 3 x 6 in. Fold one end to make it 2¹/2 in. wide. Tape the two axles to the board, one at each end. Leave space for the wheels to rotate freely.

5 Cut a piece of cardboard 3 x 14 in. Fold it over and bend it into a cab shape. Tape the two loose ends together. Stick the bottom of the cab shape to the car base.

6 Cut two cardboard shapes 6 in. long x 4 in. high. Trim them with the scissors to the same shape as the side of your car cab. Attach the sides to the cab with tape.

DECORATE YOUR CAR

You will need: two colors of acrylic paints, medium paintbrushes, pencil, 3 pieces of 6 x 8¹/2-in. colored card stock, 1 piece of white card stock, two colors of felt-tipped pens, scissors, glue.

1 Remove the wheels from your car. Paint the sides and top of the cab with one of the two colors of paint. Paint two coats and let dry.

2 Draw exciting designs for the sides of the car, and a driver to go behind the windshield. Color them in with the felt-tipped pens.

4 Replace the wheels when they are dry. Now your car looks just like a real street machine. Cut photographs of cars from magazines for ideas for new designs.

3 Let the paint dry for a couple of hours. Cut the designs out of the card stock. Glue them to the sides and back of the car. Paint the wheels with the color of paint not yet used.

FRICTION AND OIL

WHEN THE parts of an engine move, they touch and create friction (rub against one another). The more quickly and often they move, the more friction there is. This makes the engine parts grow hot, but if they become too hot they expand and no longer fit properly. When this happens, the parts jam against one another and the engine seizes up.

Oil, a slippery liquid, lubricates the car engine. It is stored in the oil pan, from where it is pumped onto the moving parts. Eventually the oil gets dirty with soot and bits of dirt from outside. The dirty oil must be drained, and clean oil put in at regular intervals. Ball bearings help other moving parts of the car turn against each other. The project shows you how marbles can behave like ball bearings to reduce friction.

Oil giant

Car ownership grew steadily in the 1930s. This created a big demand for new car products. People wanted to keep their cars running smoothly and safely. Most of all, car owners needed engine oil that was always high quality, wherever and whenever they bought it. Oil companies spent a lot of money on advertisements, telling people that their oil was the best.

Sea changes

Oil rigs drill deep into the sea-bed to find crude (natural) oil. Car lubricating oil is made from this. Pumps in the rig draw the crude oil up from the sea-bed into pipes leading to refineries on land. Impurities are removed from the crude oil in the refineries. This makes it light enough to use in car engines.

Extra Jag

High-performance sports cars such as the Jaguar E-Type of the 1960s need a particularly light oil. Otherwise their powerful engines will not run smoothly. The E-Type engine in this car has six cylinders (most car engines have four). They generate the power needed to accelerate to a top speed of 150 mph. Over time a thick oil would clog the oil lines, leading to friction and wear and tear of many engine parts.

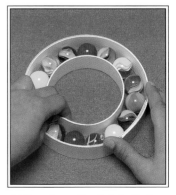

Luxury lines
Large luxury cars
need a lot of oil.
This 1958 Lincoln
Continental has a huge
8-cylinder engine to lubricate.
During the 1950s oil was very
cheap. American car makers had less reason to think about the costs
of running cars as carefully as they have in more recent years.

Beetle's brother
Between 1955 and 1974,
Karmann produced the Karmann
Ghia cabriolet for the car maker
Volkswagen. It has a special body
on the chassis (frame) of a
Volkswagen Beetle. Like the
Beetle, it has a rear engine.

BALL BEARINGS

*You will need: 8¹/2 x 11-in. sheet of
stiff card stock, scissors, tape,
5 ¹/2 x 8-in. strips of corrugated
cardboard, 16 glass marbles.*

1 Cut two strips of stiff card stock,
both ¹/2 in. wide. The first one
should be 8 in. long and the second
4 in. long. Make both into circle
shapes. Tape the ends together.

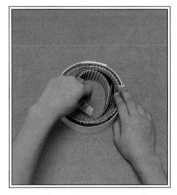

2 Use the strips of corrugated
cardboard to line the inside of
the larger card stock circle. Put all
five strips in, and make sure that they
are packed very closely together.

3 Place the smaller circle inside.
Try to turn it against the
corrugated cardboard. The
corrugations create friction so it is
not easy to turn the smaller circle.

4 Take the smaller circle and the
corrugated strips out of the large
circle. Now line the inside of the
larger circle with the marbles until
there are no gaps between them.

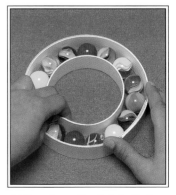

5 Place the smaller circle inside the
larger one again. Turn the small
circle. It moves very easily. The
smooth surface of the glass marbles
creates much less friction.

CLASSIC MODELS

IFFERENT PEOPLE collect different kinds of cars. Those who are looking for style collect classic cars (built after 1930, and at least twenty years old). Often the cars come from the 1950s, 1960s and 1970s. Owners take pride in the exceptional design and quality of the vehicles. For example, Rolls-Royces of any era look distinctive, and their engines and other mechanical parts were made with unusual care and the very best materials. High-performance classic sports cars such as the 1954 Mercedes-Benz Gullwing, the 1968 Aston Martin DB4, the 1960s Ford Mustang and the 1988 Porsche 959 are popular, too.

Collectors of classic cars often belong to specialized clubs. The clubs help them to find the spare parts needed for their cars and to meet people who are interested in the same models. Motor museums such as the Museum of Automobile History, the National Motor Museum in the United Kingdom and the Porsche Museum in Germany exhibit classic cars for people to look at and enjoy.

One of the greats
Few sports cars are as eagerly collected as the 1949 Jaguar XK120. It combines high speed with good looks. Its six-cylinder engine has double overhead camshafts (to control the valves in the cylinder heads). It can reach speeds of up to 120 mph.

Bumper beauty
American car makers of the 1950s such as Cadillac created cars that shone with large areas of chrome (shiny metal). Bumpers and radiator grilles were molded into streamlined shapes to catch the eye.

Fly me to the Moon
The Mercedes-Benz 300SL sports car was built by hand, so only 1,400 of them were ever made The car has one very striking feature. Its passenger and driver doors open upward from the roof of the car. The unusual design gave the car its nickname "The Gullwing," because the open doors look like a seagull. It is not very easy to get in and out of the car. Once inside, the driver and passenger sit close to the ground. The engine of the Gullwing was also set very low, to make sure that the driver could see over the top of the long hood.

Air-cooled cool

The 911 series Porsche Carrera was first made in 1964. The Porsche first appeared in 1939, as a higher-powered, streamlined, variation of the Volkswagen Beetle. Like the Beetle, the Porsche engine was air-cooled. Then, in 1997, the firm produced its first water-cooled car, the 928.

Classic car, classic film

The 1997 film comedy *Austin Powers* used many different examples of 1960s style. They all helped to recreate the fun-loving, swinging image of that period. In this scene, the hero of the film, played by Mike Myers, is standing up in the seat of a 1960s Jaguar E-Type. The bullet shape of this car is a classic design of the period.

Lucky devil

Italian car maker Lamborghini produces the classic cars of tomorrow. They are are among the world's most exotic and expensive cars. This 1990 Diablo (devil) can accelerate to 60 mph in just four seconds.

Classic performance

The British car maker Jaguar made many classic models in the past, such as the XK120 and the E-Type. The cars it makes today are also of top quality and performance. This 150-mph XKR convertible's engine is supercharged to give extra power.

Super-streamlined

Modern sports-car maker Marcos designs cars such as the Mantis that are destined to become classics of the future. They have luxurious interiors and powerful engines to match any of the old greats. The streamlining on the front of this Mantis gives the car a look that stands out from other sports cars.

SPORTS CARS

SPORTS CARS, also known as roadsters, are made for speed, not comfort. Their engines are more powerful than those in everyday cars. In addition, they usually have only two seats. That way they carry less weight than ordinary cars. A French Delage super-sports car made an international record in 1932 with a speed of 110 mph. In 1996, the British Lotus Esprit V8 arrived on the scene with a top speed of 170 mph. Sports cars are driven on ordinary roads but they can also be driven in races. The 1972 Italian Lancia Stratos won the Monte Carlo Rally five times. The engines and bodies of sports cars are often developed from race cars and have been tested under tough conditions. The Le Mans 24-hour race in France is used as a gruelling testing ground for sports car engines.

Breezing along
A 1904 Mercedes was no car to drive if you caught colds easily. There was no such thing as a convertible (a car with a folding roof) in 1904. But this Mercedes was still built for speed. A restored model shows the beautiful headlights and coachwork (bodywork) created for this masterpiece of early car engineering.

Friend of frogeye
This is a Big Healey, one of the larger models produced by the British car maker Austin Healey. The company are also known for their small sports car, the Sprite, nicknamed Frogeye because of its bulbous headlights. Austin Healey ceased production in 1971, but their cars are favorites with collectors.

FACT BOX

- Jaguar produced their first sports car, the SS90, in 1935.

- The 1968 Aston Martin DB5 was the favorite car of James Bond

- The Chevrolet Camaro was first produced in 1967 and is a powerful sports car, still popular today among collectors. The 1989 model had a V-8 engine that could reach 150 mph.

- The MG sports cars are so-called because the company that made them was originally called Morris Garages.

Red bullet
The 1961 Jaguar E-Type's engine was developed from the one used in Jaguar's D-Type race cars. Jaguar regularly took part in race car events in the 1950s. The D-Type was a truly great race car. It won the Le Mans 24-hour race four times between 1953 and 1957.

Pushy Porsche

The rear wing sticking out of the back of the Porsche 911 Turbo improves the flow of air over the back of the car when it travels at high speed. It works by flattening out the air flow as it moves over the top of the car and down the rear. This helps to keep the car's body firmly on the road and the driver in control on tight curves.

Cool bug

The Volkswagen Beetle was developed as an inexpensive family car. Then the 1968 Cabriolet appeared and surprised everyone. Volkswagen had made the engine more powerful to bring it into the same speed range as other small sports cars. It also had a flexible roof that could roll back in hot weather. Cars like this are called convertibles. This sporty Beetle is one of many changes the design has gone through since it was first produced in 1939.

Silver speeder

The Bugatti company started building high-quality sports and race cars in 1909, first in Germany and then in France. When the firm was sold in 1956, people feared it would never make cars again. In 1991, however, the Bugatti EB110 appeared, hoping to keep the glory of the past alive. Its design, 12-valve engine and four-wheel drive were praised widely. In 1994 Bugatti closed again, but the company was later bought by Volkswagen.

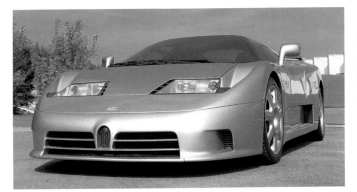

Beautiful beamer

The BMW (*Bayerische Motoren Werke*) company has made cars and motorcycles in the German city of Munich since 1928. In the 1970s, they began to sell more of their cars outside Germany. By the 1980s, BMWs were popular throughout the world. Although this 3-series convertible from the 1990s has four seats, its 115-mph top speed means it is still seen as a two-door sports car.

FUEL CONTROL

THE CONTROLLED flow of fuel into a car's engine is very important, because it affects how the car performs. If there is too much fuel and not enough air, the engine floods with gasoline and will not start. If there is not enough fuel, the engine will run in a jerky way. The mixing of fuel and air occurs inside the carburetor. A piston goes down as a valve opens to let the fuel and air mixture in. The valve closes and the piston goes up, compressing (squeezes) the fuel and air mixture. The spark plug fires to ignite the fuel mixture, pushing the piston down again. The piston rises again and the exhaust valve opens to release the waste gases.

The project shows you how to make a model that works in the same way as the camshaft. It opens one valve and then, as it closes the first valve, a second valve opens.

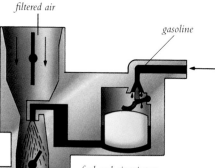

filtered air

gasoline

fuel and air mixture

Mixing it
In cold weather, engines need more fuel to get started. In some cars the driver pulls out a choke. This causes the carburetor to increase the amount of fuel in the fuel and air mixture. Many modern cars have automatic chokes. Internal computers work out the exact mixture of fuel and air that will suit the weather conditions.

Double trouble
Very powerful cars such as the Lamborghini Diablo need to generate a lot of energy to accelerate (increase speed) quickly. They have 12 cylinders in their engines, burning much more fuel than an ordinary 4-cylinder car. The burned fuel creates a large amount of exhaust gas. The Diablo has four exhaust pipes at the rear of the car. Most ordinary cars have only one exhaust pipe.

ROCK AND ROLL CAMSHAFT

You will need: scissors, 2¹/2-in. square stiff card stock, masking tape, cardboard tube with plastic lid, pencil.

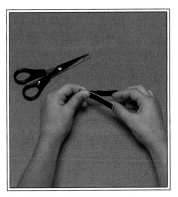

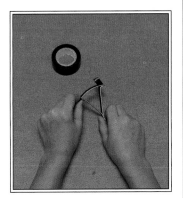

1 Use scissors to cut a ¹/2 x 2¹/2-in. strip from the stiff card stock. Fold it over in the center. Hold it with your fingertips. Bend the two ends of the card stock away from one another.

2 Cut a ¹/2 x 1¹/2-in. strip from the original piece of card stock. Use masking tape to fix the card strip to the folded bottom ends of the first piece. This makes a triangle shape.

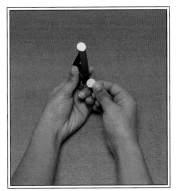

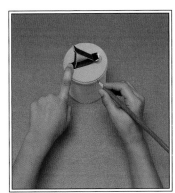

3 Use the scissors to cut out two small circle shapes from the original piece of card stock. Use masking tape to secure them to the bottom piece of the triangle you have made.

4 Put the triangle on top of the cardboard tube. The circles should touch the plastic lid. With a pencil, mark where the circles sit on the lid.

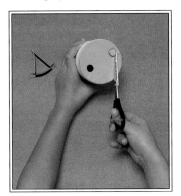

5 Using the scissors, carefully cut around the pencil marks you have made in the plastic lid of the tube. These form an inlet and an outlet.

6 Now you can rock the triangle back and forth to cover and uncover the two holes one after another. This is just how a camshaft opens and shuts the intake and exhaust valves in a car's cylinder.

SUSPENSION

THE EARLIEST cars used coach wheels made of wood and metal. They provided a very bumpy ride. In the early 1900s, the French company Michelin made a rubber tire with an inflatable inner tube. The idea came from the inner tube tire that John Dunlop developed in the late 1800s for bicycles. The outer part of the tire was made of rubber. Inside it had a tube filled with air. The air cushioned the car's contact with the road and driving became much more comfortable. All car tires had inner tubes until the 1950s. From then on, more tubeless tires were made. In these, air is held in a web of cords and an inner tire that fits very tightly on the wheel rim. Cars use suspension systems, as well as air-filled tires, as cushioning. Suspension systems are attached to a car's wheels to absorb impacts from the road. In modern cars these are usually either coiled springs, shaped rubber cones or gas-filled cylinders.

Thick and thin
The engines on hot rods (cars with boosted engines) drive the rear wheels. These wheels often have thick tires. This means there is a lot of contact between the road surface and the tire surface, helping the car to grip the road when accelerating.

Suspension
A car's suspension system makes driving comfortable. It prevents the car from being bumped up and down too much on bumpy roads. In the early 1900s, car suspension was the same as the suspension in horse-drawn carriages. Modern cars use much more sophisticated systems. The Jaguar XKR Coupe shown here has a coiled spring system. The suspension system is attached to each wheel. If the car goes over a 2-in. bump, the wheel will go up 2 in. too, but the car's body will move up less distance. The suspension system absorbs the impact. After going over the bump, the car's body will sink down slowly, too. Hydraulic cylinders (cylinders full of a liquid or gas, such as oil) do this. The cylinders are called dampers, because they damp down the effect of the bump.

Taking off

Rally cars travel so quickly that when they come over the top of a hill they can leave the ground for a second or two. Then they come back down to earth with a stomach-churning bump. A hard landing can shatter a car's axles and put the car out of the competition. Rally cars take this kind of punishment hour after hour, day after day. They have to be fitted with extra-strong suspension systems

Early tires

A 1903 Mercedes-Benz sports car is equipped with tires made of rubber casing. Inside these were rubber tubes filled with air, just like the inner tubes in bicycle tires. Tire manufacturers stopped including inner tubes in car tires from the 1950s onward. Drivers were having too many flats.

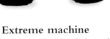

Extreme machine

Four truck wheels have hijacked a pickup truck to provide a well-cushioned ride. In the quest for ever more bizarre effects, someone has put a pickup truck on top of a metal frame. The frame is then specially linked to the type of tires normally seen on enormous road vehicles such as earth-moving trucks. Suspension on this scale allows the truck to travel over extremely uneven surfaces, such as an uneven quarry floor.

Big smoothie

Limousines look spectacular and provide exceptional levels of comfort. Stretch limousines are the most luxurious of all. They are often used for weddings and other important events. Very long cars like this have what is known as SRC (Selective Ride Control) suspension to make for an extra-smooth ride. Computers control chambers filled with gas that is pressurized by a pump. The compressed air absorbs shocks from the road.

HOME FROM HOME

THE GREAT advantage of setting off on an adventure by car is that you can go where you want, when you want. It is even possible to travel to places where there may be no towns or people. Once you're there, however, what do you do when you want to go to sleep at night? One solution is to drive a special car such as a multi-purpose vehicle (MPV) or a recreational vehicle (RV). They are built to provide sleeping space. Smaller ones have car seats that will lie flat to make a bed. Larger RVs have cabins with built-in bunks, kitchens and sitting areas. They may also have televisions, music systems, microwave ovens and all the high-tech equipment that can be found in a conventional house. The interiors of top-of-the-range RVs can be built according to the buyer's preferences.

Long way from home
Long-distance truck drivers, who drive thousands of miles every year, often travel through regions where there are very few towns or villages. At night the driver finds a safe place to park, then sleeps in a built-in bunk behind the driver's seat.

Time for a drink
Rolls-Royce built the 1960 Phantom as a touring car for people who wanted to travel to the countryside and eat when they arrived. The small seats fold down when the car is moving and pull up in front of the liquor cabinet when the car is stopped. Cars like this were often driven to outdoor events such as horse races, where eating a picnic from a car is a tradition.

Open-air life
Campers are mobile living units that can be towed from place to place by cars. Towing a camper requires a lot of extra power from the car, so larger vehicles are the most suitable. Drivers have to keep their speed down when pulling a camper, because the camper could easily flip over.

SCENTED CAR AIR FRESHENER

You will need: *7 oz water, mixing bowl, 1 cup all-purpose flour, wooden spoon, baking sheet, pencil, bottle of essential oil, paintbrush, four colors of acrylic paint, 18-in length of string.*

1 Pour the water into a mixing bowl. Stir in the flour slowly with a wooden spoon. Continue to stir until the paste thickens into a dough mixture that you can mold.

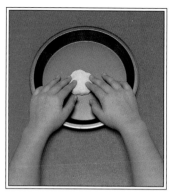

2 Place the dough mixture on a baking sheet. Mold the dough into a bell shape that bulges out at the bottom. Roughly shape a roof at the top and wheels underneath.

3 Wet the rough shape so it is easy to mold a design on it. Smooth your fingers over the top area to make a windshield. Shape the wheels more accurately.

4 Make small holes in the car and one larger hole in the top. Sprinkle essential oil in the holes. Bake in an oven for 45 minutes at 300°F. Let cool.

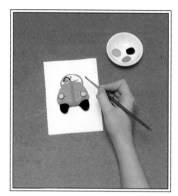

5 Once the car is cool, place it on a sheet of paper. Paint the hood first, then the details, such as a driver's face. Add lines around the headlights.

6 Allow the paint to dry. Thread the piece of string through the hole in the top of the car's windshield. Double the string back and knot it to make a noose.

7 Your air freshener is all ready to go in a real car. Now you can put it on the dashboard, hang it from the back of a seat or put it on the shelf in front of the rear window. It will make any car smell fresh and clean.

FUEL CONSUMPTION

THE AMOUNT of gasoline a car uses depends on the weight of the car, the speed it is traveling, and the size and efficiency of the engine. Pressing on the accelerator pedal lets more fuel flow into the engine's cylinders, speeding the car up. Most ordinary cars have four cylinders. A few extremely economical cars have two cylinders, and some powerful cars have six or even eight. Today, cars of all engine size are designed to use as little fuel as possible. This is because the oil from which gasoline is made is much more expensive than it was in the 1950s and 1960s. The average modern car can travel 35 to 50 mph on one gallon of gas. Gas guzzlers such as the Cadillac Fleetwood could only drive 10 miles on a gallon of gas.

Roaring oldie
Super Street hot rodders often take the bodies of old cars and combine them with modern parts. The 1950s car body here has been joined to big tires by a complicated suspension system. Some hot rodders use special chemical fuels such as ethanol and nitromethane. When they burn, they get much hotter than gasoline. The extra heat helps them to accelerate to very high speeds.

FACT BOX

• Rising oil prices in the late 1900s led to the creation of gasohol, a mixture of lead-free gasoline and ethanol. Ethanol can be made from plants such as grain and potatoes.

• Traces of the metal lead in car exhaust fumes are harmful. It is thought that many people suffered lead poisoning. Now, lead-free gasoline has been developed and is widely available.

Where's the car?
Members of the Eddie Jordan pitstop crew swarm over the Jordan 199 at the Australian Grand Prix in 1999. In the center, a team member holds the hose that forces fuel into the car's gas tank at high pressure. Up to 25 gals of fuel can be pumped into the car in about 10 seconds. Speed is essential. Every second in the pit lane is equal to about 60 yds lost on the track.

Two-carb Caddy

The Cadillacs of the 1950s are reminders of a time when gasoline was cheap and car makers could make big, heavy cars. In the 1970s, the price of oil rose dramatically, so gas became much more expensive. The 1955 Cadillac Fleetwood had two carburetors, even though most cars built at that time would have had just one. The second carburetor was needed because the Fleetwood used so much gasoline.

Pink Thunderbird

The sleek rear fins and supercool spare-wheel holder made the 1957 Ford Thunderbird a car that people remembered long after Ford stopped making the model. This restored T-Bird is a convertible. When the cars were first sold, buyers were given both a hard top and a convertible top. They could use whichever one they wanted. In 1998, the 1957 Thunderbird's good looks earned it a Lifetime Automotive Design Achievement Award from the Detroit Institute of Ophthalmology.

Twice as much

Cars that use a lot of gasoline may have two or even four exhausts. Twin exhausts extract waste gases from the engine in a more efficient way than a single exhaust could, which allows the engine to perform more efficiently, too.

Flying flatbed

Flatbed trucks such as this are favorites for customizing enthusiasts. They take an old truck and turn it into an ORV (Off-Road Vehicle). An ORV consumes lots of gasoline as it drives across rough country, often far from any gas stations. They carry large cans of gas in case they run out.

SPEED RECORDS

Electric with excitement
Between December 1898 and April 1899, there were no less than six attempts to beat the land-speed record. All of them were made by drivers in electric cars. The fastest, in April, was the Belgian Camille Jenatzy who reached 65 mph. He called his car *La Jamais Contente* (Never Satisfied) because he had already tried to set the land-speed record twice before.

I N MORE than a hundred years of car building, cars have reached faster and faster speeds. In 1899, the Belgian inventor Camille Jenatzy was the first person to drive a car faster than 60 mph. The car, designed by Jenatzy himself, ran on electricity. In the same year Sir Charles Wakefield created his Castrol Motor Oil company. The company awards the official trophy for the land-speed record to drivers who break the record. The trophy was first won in 1914 by the Englishman L.G. Hornsted. He reached a speed of 175 mph in a car from the German car maker Benz. Since then 38 other people have broken the record. The last person to succeed was the RAF Tornado pilot Andy Green, on October 13, 1997. His car, powered by two jet engines, broke the sound barrier (sound travels at a speed of 760 mph reaching 761 mph.

Gas-powered wheels
Finding a long, flat, hard surface to travel on is very important when trying to set a speed record on land. Donald Campbell thundered across the Lake Eyre Salt Flats in Australia in 1964. He reached a speed of 402 mph in his gas-turbine powered car Bluebird. He was following in the footsteps of his father Malcolm, who set nine land-speed records.

Golden goer
The Golden Arrow set a land-speed record of 230 mph on March 11, 1929. The enormous, streamlined car was powered by a Napier-Lion airplane engine. It flashed along the hard, white sand at Daytona Beach, Florida. The driver was Major Henry Seagrave. After setting the land-speed record, Seagrave went on to set the World Water Speed Record.

Goodbye, Mr Bond

In the 1974 James Bond film *The Man with the Golden Gun*, the character James Bond performs many death-defying feats. His car takes at least as much punishment as the Secret Service Agent himself. To fly across the river, the car would have had to be traveling at 125 mph when taking off from the ramp.

Pushy guy

The Black Rock Desert in Nevada was the scene for another record-breaking attempt in 1983. On this dried lake bed, in blistering desert heat, Richard Noble set a new record of 631 mph. He was driving a specially made jet-engine powered Thrust 2. Making a speed record attempt costs a lot of money. The advertisements plastered all over the car are for businesses that sponsored this record attempt.

Head for the horizon

Ever since commercial movies started to be made in the early 1900s, car chases have formed part of the action. The cars are usually driven by stunt men and women specially trained in fast driving. In the 1991 film *Thelma and Louise*, shown above, the two heroines are chased by dozens of police cars. In the end, the two women drive off a cliff.

Supersonic car

In 1997 Andy Green drove the Thrust SSC at an incredible 761 mph. He did not just set a new world land-speed record, he traveled faster than the speed of sound (760 mph). Until then, speeds greater than that of sound had only been possible in flight. Andy was used to the speed because he was a jet pilot for the British Royal Air Force.

ROADS AND HIGHWAYS

BEFORE THE 1800s, most roads were just earth tracks. Some roads in cities and towns were made of stone and wood blocks, which gave a rough ride. Macadam roads (roads covered in a hard layer of tiny stones) were a great improvement in the 1800s, but with the invention of cars at the end of the 1800s, new road surfaces were needed. Roads made of asphalt (a mixture of bitumen and stone) and concrete offered the hardness and smoothness that cars needed to travel safely and quickly.

The first highway was completed in 1932 in Germany, between Cologne and Bonn. As car ownership grew during the second half of the 1900s, road building programs followed. Some people think there are too many roads. They protest against the building of more roads because they want to protect the countryside.

Multi-lane moves
Car ownership and use has grown relentlessly, and highways and freeways have grown too. In the last 30 years the freeways have increased in size from 4 lanes to 12 lanes, and even to 16 lanes on some stretches.

Pay as you go
The enormous costs of building highways can be partly paid for by charging drivers a toll (payment for using a road) when they travel on the new roads. The road owners set up barriers through which a car must pass to drive onto the road. Drivers crossing the Queen Elizabeth Bridge in Dartford, England, stop at toll booths to buy tickets that allow them to drive over the bridge.

Keep calm
Traffic calming is the name given to the different ways of slowing down traffic speed. Building speed bumps is one example of traffic calming. The speed bumps force drivers to slow down in areas where there is a lot of housing. Slower car speeds help to prevent accidents.

Going places

Modern countries need well-built roads so that goods and people can travel easily between cities and towns. This is Interstate 35 approaching Minneapolis. It is part of the vast interstate highway system that links the entire United States.

Major to minor

Road networks are often much easier to understand from the air. A cloverleaf links two major highways. Long curving roads such as these allow drivers to switch between major roads without having to stop at an intersection. The roads that link up major roads are called access roads.

Night guide

Small glass reflectors called Catseyes help drivers to see the road at night. The Catseyes are set at regular intervals in the middle of the road. They gleam brightly when a car's headlights shine on them. The British inventor Percy Shaw invented the device in 1933, after noticing how a cat's eyes shine at night.

The long and winding road

There are still many narrow old roads in remote areas. They twist and turn for miles through beautiful countryside. There is much less traffic on country roads, and they offer an enjoyable test of driving skills. Four-wheel drive vehicles handle particularly well on the tight corners and steep slopes.

Conic section

Modern roads carry a lot of traffic and need constant repair and maintenance. They cannot simply be shut down while that happens. Instead, some lanes are closed for repair while others remain open. The long lines of plastic cones on this stretch of highway have restricted traffic to one lane on one side and two lanes on the other side.

ORNAMENTS AND MASCOTS

CAR MANUFACTURERS take pride in the work that goes into the machines that they make. They put hood ornaments or symbols on their cars to show which company made the car. There are many different car makers all over the world, and they each make a different hood ornament. The instantly recognizable designs of the most prestigious companies, such as the Silver Lady on Rolls-Royces or the three-spoked circle on Mercedes cars, suggest elegance or power. Other celebrated symbols are the rearing horse on the front of cars made by the Italian Ferrari company, and the VW symbol used on Volkswagen cars. Sometimes these hood ornaments are called mascots, perhaps because car makers see them as a symbol of good luck. When people identify a car's hood ornament, they immediately know the name of the car maker. In this project, you can make your own hood ornament to symbolize the kind of car you like.

Leading lady
All Rolls-Royce cars carry a winged figure mascot on the hood. It is called The Spirit of Ecstasy and was created by the sculptor Charles Sykes. The figure first appeared on Rolls-Royce cars in 1911. In modern Rolls-Royces, the mascot folds down backward into the hood during an accident to avoid injury.

HOOD HERO

You will need: 8¹/2 x 11-in. sheet of cardboard, pencil, scissors, tape, awl, glue, matchstick, newspaper, fork, 1 cup all-purpose flour, 7 fl oz water, tin of silver spray paint, fine paintbrush, black paint.

1 Cut a piece measuring 6 x 8 in. from the cardboard. Use a pencil to draw the outline of the shape you want to put on your car hood on the cardboard sheet.

2 Use the scissors to cut roughly around the ornament shape. Then cut around the outline accurately. Be careful not to cut off any of the detail in your drawing.

3 Cut three square pieces from the cardboard, one 2 in., one 2¹/2 in. and one 3 in. Tape the smallest on top of the next largest and those on top of the largest as a solid base.

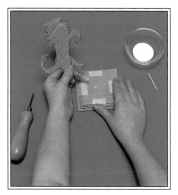

4 Make a hole in the center of the base with the awl. Put a glued matchstick in the bottom of your ornament. Insert it into the hole in the base so the ornament stands upright.

5 Tear strips of newspaper. Mix flour and water to make a thick paste. Use your fingers to dip the paper in the mixture. Apply the wet paper to the ornament in three layers.

6 When the newspaper is dry, spray your ornament with spray paint. Be careful to point the can downward, away from you. Put a piece of paper under the ornament.

7 Use the paintbrush to apply black lines on the ornament where you want to show more detail. For example, this one shows detail of the lion's mane, tail and paws.

Speeder's shield

The ornament on Porsche cars is like a coat of arms from medieval times. In the past, important people made decorations on shield shapes to tell others who their ancestors were and where they came from.

8 Your finished ornament could form the start of a great collection. You could copy all your favorite car ornaments. There are many more to choose from.

Roar of power
Jaguar cars have used the model of the leaping jaguar as their hood ornament for many years. More recent models do not have the statuette on the hood. They have been declared illegal because they could cause injury to pedestrians in an accident.

THE FUTURE

THE CARS of the future already exist, but only as the unrevealed designs of car makers. The use of in-car computers will be one of the main ways in which cars will change. These already control engine performance, navigation aids and air temperature. In future, a computer chip may apply the brakes automatically when the car in front is too close, or flash up HUDs (Heads Up Display) messages on the windshield about road conditions ahead.

Designers and engineers will continue to develop fuel-efficient cars (ones that use as little gasoline as possible), such as the Toyota Echo. They will also look at the potential of alternative power sources such as electricity, natural gas (a gas found underground), solar power (power from the sun's energy) and hydrogen (a gas in the earth's atmosphere). Of all the many developments that will occur, one is almost certain. There will be even more cars on the roads.

Hot item
Cars powered by energy from the sun (solar power) would be better for the environment than gas-powered cars. Photo-electric cells on the back of the car turn energy from the sun's rays into electricity. This energy is stored in batteries inside the car. The batteries then supply power to the engine. At the moment this method can only store enough energy to power small cars. Scientists are trying to find a way to use solar power in bigger vehicles.

FACT BOX

• The American car manufacturer General Motors is developing a car that will change its shape from a sedan to a pickup truck by means of voice-activated commands spoken by the driver in the front seat.

• Car makers are building concept (future idea) cars in which each seat has its own LCD (liquid-crystal display) screen. Passengers will be able to send and receive e-mail, browse the internet, make phone calls and read maps.

Take me home
GPS (Global Positioning System) navigation aids are already standard features in top-range cars. A radio antenna in the car sends a signal to one of the 24 GPS satellites that orbit the earth. The satellite sends a signal back to the car giving its exact position on the earth. The data is sent to a computer that reads maps stored on a CD-ROM. A small screen on the dashboard of the car displays a map of the road network and the position of the car on the map. If the driver inputs the destination, the screen displays the best route.

Neat package

Car makers produced classic microcars such as the BMW Isetta in the 1950s and 1960s. In the future, they will continue to make very small cars. They are ideal for short journeys in developed areas. The number of cars in towns and cities continues to grow. Extra-small vehicles such as the Smart car could be the answer to parking problems. It is so short (8 ft) that it can park not just along the edge of the road, but facing the sidewalk.

Snappy mover

Research has shown that on most journeys, the average number of people who travel in a car is two. Car makers now know that two-seater cars like the one shown here make a lot of sense for many drivers. Less metal is needed to make them, they use less fuel, and they are cheaper to buy. A car as small as this is also much easier to maneuver in the tight spaces of modern cities.

Three-wheel dream

One-person cars seem an obvious answer to many traffic problems. They are not always a hit with drivers, however. The British inventor Sir Clive Sinclair produced the electric-powered Sinclair C5 in 1985. The vehicle was not very popular, and was soon taken out of production.

Future taxi

Will the four-wheel yellow cabs of New York today be replaced by three-wheel taxis in the future? The 1992 science-fiction film *Freejack* showed great imagination in guessing what the taxicabs of tomorrow might look like.

GLOSSARY

accelerator pedal
The pedal beneath the driver's foot that controls the flow of fuel to a car engine.

air cooled
An engine in which the heat is carried away, not by water, but by air.

air pollution
The reduction of the oxygen content in the air we breath with poisonous gases such as carbon monoxide.

airbag
A cushion stored in front of car seats that automatically inflates in a crash, protecting the driver and passengers.

all-terrain vehicles (ATVs)
Cars that are built for driving on rough surfaces such as unpaved roads.

amphibious car
A car that travels on land and in water.

antilock braking systems (ABS)
A specially designed braking system that avoids wheels locking and skidding when the brakes are applied.

asphalt
A mixture of bitumen and concrete used to give roads a hard, smooth, weatherproof surface.

ball bearing
A hardened steel ball, often arranged with other ball bearings around a turning surface to ease movement.

battery
A container of chemicals holding a charge of electricity.

bodywork
The outside body of a car.

brake
A pad or disc that slows a moving surface down by pressing it.

bubble car
The name given in the 1950s and 1960s to microcars such as the BMW Isetta, because of their round shape.

bumper
The protective, wraparound metal or rubber barrier that protects the front and rear of a car.

cabriolet
A car with a flexible roof that can be folded away into the rear of the car.

camshaft
A shaft, driven and timed with the engine crankshaft. Lobes rotate on the camshaft, opening and closing the inlet and exhaust valves in the cylinder head.

carbon monoxide
A poisonous gas that is a by-product of burning gasoline.

carburetor
A unit that controls the fuel mixture entering the combustion chamber.

checkered flag
A black-and-white square patterned flag that an official waves as a car crosses the finishing line in a race.

chrome
A reflective metal used to cover car parts such as bumpers and radiator grilles to make them look shiny.

classic car
A car that, because of special qualities of design and workmanship, is collected and restored.

convertible
A car that can be driven with and without a roof.

crankshaft
The part that transmits the four-stroke movement of the pistons to the car's driveline and road wheels.

custom car
A car that has been deliberately adapted by its owner to make it look and drive the way he or she wants.

cylinder
A hollow tube in which a piston moves.

dashboard
The vertical surface that contains the instruments facing a driver inside a car.

drag racer
A car specially designed to take part in short, high-speed acceleration races.

flatbed
A small truck with a driver's cab in the front and an open, horizontal platform at the rear.

Formula One
The class of racing car that has the most powerful engine specification.

four-wheel drive
A car in which power from the engine can be transferred to all four wheels, not just to the front or rear wheels.

friction
The rubbing of one surface against another surface.

fuel
A substance, such as gasoline, that is burned to provide energy.

fuel efficient
A car that is designed to use as little fuel as possible while ensuring normal speed and power.

gases
Non-solid, non-liquid substances given off when gasoline burns.

gasoline
The easily burned liquid made from oil that is the main fuel for internal combustion engines.

gear
A toothed wheel designed to interact with other toothed wheels to transfer motion in a controlled way.

highway
A specially built, wide road, often with between 6 and 12 lanes, designed to allow large amounts of traffic to travel long distances at speed.

hot rod
A car in which the engine has been specially treated to allow it to accelerate rapidly and travel at high speed.

hydraulic
Worked by the pressure of fluid carried in pipes.

inner tube
A rubber tube filled with air contained inside the tires of older vehicles.

internal combustion
The burning of fuel in a closed chamber to generate power.

limousine
A particularly large, luxurious car.

lubrication
The smoothing of friction between the parts of an engine, usually with oil.

microcar
A particularly small car, designed for use in cities to minimize traffic congestion.

mudguard
The wide wing of metal around a car wheel that prevents mud and stones from flying up off the road.

multi-purpose vehicle (MPV)
A car that has more than one use, for example, one that can carry as many passengers as a small van.

off-road vehicle (ORV)
A car that can drive on surfaces other than smooth, paved roads.

oil
A thick, black liquid found under the surface of the Earth from which gasoline and other products can be made.

pedestrian
A person who travels on foot.

pickup
A small truck with a cab at the front and a flat platform over the rear wheels.

production line
A way of manufacturing machines in which all the parts are added one by one in a continuous process in a factory.

prototype
The first attempt to build a working model of a machine from the design.

radiator
A container of water from which water is pumped around the engine to prevent overheating.

recreational vehicle (RV)
A combination car and camper, with living and sleeping accommodations.

robot
A machine that is built to perform particular tasks automatically.

rubber
A liquid taken from rubber trees that, when treated, forms a thick, flexible material suitable for making tires.

seat belt
A safety strap worn by drivers and passengers to prevent injury in the case of an accident.

speedometer
The dial on a car's dashboard that displays the speed at which the car is traveling.

sports car
A car designed for speed rather than comfort, often with only two seats.

steam engine
An engine powered by the steam (water vapor) created by heating water.

steering mechanism
The combined system of steering wheel, rack and pinion mechanism and wheels that allows a driver to steer a car.

stock car
An ordinary car that has been adapted to make it suitable for racing.

streamlining
Shaping a car's body so that it can travel with low air resistance.

suspension system
The springs and other shock absorbers that cushion the movement of a car's wheels on the road.

veteran car
Any car built before 1905.

vintage car
Any car built between 1919 and 1930.

wind tunnel
A large chamber in which powerful drafts of air are blown over a car to test and measure how much air resistance the car shows.

Index